LEGENDS OF WARFARE

AVIATION

Grumman J2F Duck

US Navy, Marine Corps, Army Air Force, and Coast Guard Use in World War II

DAVID DOYLE

Schiffer Publishing Ltd

4880 Lower Valley Road • Atglen, PA 19310

Designed by Justin Watkinson
Type set in Impact/Minion Pro/Univers LT Std

ISBN: 978-0-7643-5448-9
Printed in China

Published by Schiffer Publishing, Ltd.
4880 Lower Valley Road
Atglen, PA 19310
Phone: (610) 593-1777; Fax: (610) 593-2002
E-mail: Info@schifferbooks.com
www.schifferbooks.com

For our complete selection of fine books on this and related subjects, please visit our website at www.schifferbooks.com. You may also write for a free catalog.

Schiffer Publishing's titles are available at special discounts for bulk purchases for sales promotions or premiums. Special editions, including personalized covers, corporate imprints, and excerpts can be created in large quantities for special needs. For more information, contact the publisher.

We are always looking for people to write books on new and related subjects. If you have an idea for a book, please contact us at proposals@schifferbooks.com.

Acknowledgments

As with all of my projects, this book would not have been possible without the generous help of many friends. Noted aviation photographers Rich Kolasa and Bill Scheuerman provided many of the photographs, including some impressive aerial photos. Also instrumental to the completion of this book were Tom Kailbourn, Scott Taylor, Leo Polaski, as well as Stan Piet with the Glenn L. Martin Maryland Aviation Museum; Brett Stolle with the National Museum of the United States Air Force; and the staff of the National Museum of Naval Aviation. Most importantly, a thank you to my wife Denise, for her unflagging support.

Contents

Introduction

Grumman constructed a wooden mock-up of the prototype of the Duck, the XJF-1, complete with landing gear. This photo shows the locations of the pilot and, behind him, the gunner/observer. Bulkheads and some of the frame members were indicated. *Grumman Memorial Park*

In another view of the mock-up of the prototype, the gunner is standing up and manning his .30-caliber machine gun. The Duck had provisions for transporting up to two passengers in the float, as indicated by the two men seated below the gunner. *Grumman Memorial Park*

The story of the Duck, and indeed all Grumman aircraft, begins with Loening Aeronautical Engineering—an enterprise formed by Grover Loening, who had persuaded talented naval aviator Leroy Grumman to resign his commission and join his firm. Noted for their amphibians, in 1928, the company merged with Keystone Aircraft, creating Keystone-Loening. In 1929, this firm was taken over by Curtiss-Wright, who proceeded to relocate the company, much to the dismay of several key employees. Those employees, led by Leroy Grumman, Jake Swirbul, William Schwendler, Julius Holpit, and Albert Loening, left and formed the Grumman Aircraft Engineering Corporation. The new company was completely and privately financed by Grover Loening, who also provided the manufacturing rights to the Loening retractable landing gear, hull, and float designs.

These rights led directly to the development of the Grumman Model A and Model B floats, which equipped the Vought 02U and 03U observation aircraft, and provided the fledgling firm with the first of the many US Navy contracts that would make the company famous.

Loening had built a reputation in the 1920s for their amphibians, and some of these had made their way into the hands of the US military, becoming the Air Corps's OA series and the Navy's OL series. At the outset of the 1930s, the Navy desired to replace these aircraft with improved models, to be designated "J" for transport. With the Navy's encouragement, the Loening XO2L-1 was redesigned by the Grumman firm, becoming what was known internally as the Grumman Design 7. The Navy ordered a prototype of the redesigned aircraft, and designated it the XJF-1. The Navy would soon have its first Duck.

CHAPTER 1
XJF-1

Grumman XJF-1 BuNo 9218, or Grumman Design 7, was a one-off prototype of an amphibious biplane. It was a redesign of the Grover Loening XO2L-1; Grumman took over development of the design when it became apparent that the Grover Loening Aircraft Company lacked the factory capacity to produce the aircraft should the prototype go into full production. The Navy ordered the XJF-1 in 1932, and Paul Hovgard was the pilot on the aircraft's first flight, conducted from the airfield at Grumman's Farmingdale, Long Island, plant on April 24, 1933. *National Archives and Records Administration*

Navy contract 26467 called for the construction of a single prototype of the new design, which was assigned Bureau Number 9218. The aircraft would be powered by a Pratt & Whitney R-1535-62 engine developing 700 horsepower, turning a three-blade Hamilton Standard propeller. Provisions were made for carrying two 100-pound bombs on wing racks, and a flexible-mount .30-caliber machine gun for self-defense in the aft cockpit.

The XJF-1 first flew at Farmingdale on April 24, 1933, with Paul Hovgard at the controls. On May 4, 1933, it was delivered to the Navy at Naval Air Station Anacostia. Initial testing revealed a lack of longitudinal stability, and the aircraft was returned to

Grumman for correction. Various redesigns of the fin were tried, with ultimately a much larger tail being designed. With the new tail in place, the aircraft was returned to the Navy in January 1934, and was accepted for service shortly thereafter.

The XJF-1, which had a maximum speed of 164 mph and a service ceiling of 21,500 feet, had a short service life. Assigned to Naval Air Station Norfolk after acceptance, the aircraft was lost in a crash in the James River on March 8, 1934. Worse, test pilots Lt. William P. Davis and Aviation Machinist's Mate 2nd Class Matt David Marshall died in the crash.

The XJF-1 featured a large center float faired into the belly of the fuselage and a wing float under each of the lower wings. A retractable main landing gear and a non-retracting tail wheel were incorporated into the center float. On each side of the float-fuselage fairing was a large, rectangular window for the passengers. The pilot's and gunner's cockpits were entirely covered by a clear canopy. Grumman delivered the XJF-1 to the US Navy on May 4, 1933, and the plane underwent flight testing at NAS Anacostia, District of Columbia. *National Archives and Records Administration*

The XJF-1 was powered by an ungeared Pratt & Whitney R-1830-63 14-cylinder radial engine. The propeller was a three-bladed Hamilton Standard. The main landing gear retracted into recesses in the sides of the center float with just the wheels showing. *National Archives and Records Administration*

In a frontal view of the Grumman XJF-1, most likely taken at Grumman's Farmingdale, Long Island, plant in April 1933, the width of the fairing between the fuselage and the center float is apparent. The wing floats hung relatively close to the bottom wing. *National Archives and Records Administration*

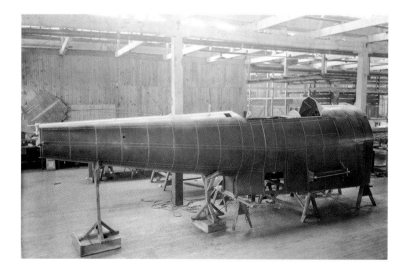

The fuselage of the XJF-1 during construction is viewed from the starboard side. The skin of the fuselage was of riveted aluminum alloy construction. Forward of the opening for the starboard passenger's window is the mount for the lower starboard wing. *National Archives and Records Administration*

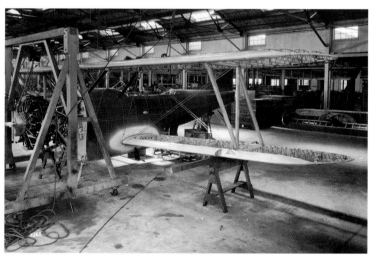

During construction of the XJF-1, as observed from the port side, the Pratt & Whitney R-1830-63 engine has been mounted, and the wings are in place, although the fabric skin had yet to be applied to the frames of the wings. The pilot's windscreen is installed. *National Archives and Records Administration*

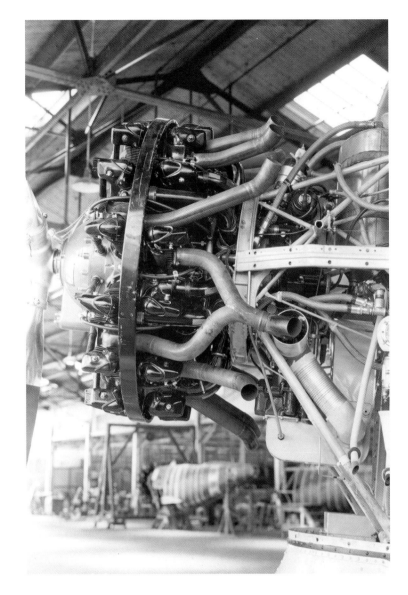

The center float of the Grumman XJF-1, also referred to as the hull structure, is viewed from the port side during construction. At the center of the float is the port landing gear bay. The patterns of the rivets that secure the skin panels in place are visible. *National Archives and Records Administration*

The Pratt & Whitney R-1830-63 of the XJF-1 is viewed from the port side with the engine cowl not yet installed. Engine exhausts protrude to the rear. Later, production versions of the Grumman Duck would eliminate the individual exhaust outlets in favor of routing the exhausts into collector rings with several exhaust outlets. Aft of the engine, some of the engine accessories are visible. *National Archives and Records Administration*

The landing-gear assemblies have been installed on the center float or hull structure of the XJF-1 in this view from the starboard side. The fairing has been completed, including the main landing gear bay. Above the top of the float, the top of the fuel tank is in view. *National Archives and Records Administration*

A Grumman factory worker poses at the flexible .30-caliber machine gun in the aft cockpit. The light colored object below the front of the barrel was a barrel lock. The circular opening on the bottom of the fuselage toward the lower left was a flare chute. *National Archives and Records Administration*

During acceptance tests at NAS Anacostia, the Navy discovered that the XJF-1 suffered from longitudinal instability. To remedy this problem, Grumman installed an enlarged vertical tail with a stepped profile owing to a vertical fin that was lower than the rudder. The vertical fin now assumed a nearly square shape, with a slightly rounded upper front corner. The shape of the rudder remained unchanged. The Bureau Number, 9218, was stenciled on the vertical fin, and the model number, XJF-1, was on the rudder. *Glenn L. Martin Maryland Aviation Museum*

The XJF-1 had provisions for bomb racks suspended from four streamlined mounts underneath the lower wings. Mounted on this rack are five Mk.V 30-pound fragmentation bombs; they are stenciled "EMPTY," meaning they were inert. *National Archives and Records Administration*

Factory workers gather around the Grumman XJF-1 as it rests on the ground at Grumman's Farmingdale, Long Island, plant. The pilot's sliding canopy has been moved back to its stored position above the fixed canopy section to the rear of his seat. *Grumman Memorial Park*

Even before the XJF-1's tragic crash, the Navy had ordered twenty-seven production examples of the type designated the JF-1. Unlike the prototype, these aircraft would be powered by the Pratt & Whitney R-1830-62 Twin Wasp. Bureau Numbers 9434 through 9455 and 9523 through 9527 were assigned to the aircraft.

The entire production run was assigned to utility squadrons, with the first operational JF-1 arriving at Naval Air Station Norfolk in May 1934. In addition to Naval Air Stations like Norfolk, the new aircraft were also dispatched to Fleet Air Bases, carrier-based utility units, and the USMC.

The first JF-1 delivered to the Marines was Bureau Number 9449, delivered on September 6, 1934. This was followed by additional aircraft, such that in time five Marine squadrons had the type on roster.

The JF-1 was the first production model of the Grumman Duck, with production beginning in 1934. The JF-1 was similar to the XJF-1 after the prototype had received its final modification to the vertical tail, in which the rudder and nearly square vertical fin had been replaced by an entirely redesigned rudder and vertical fin. Grumman delivered twenty-seven JF-1s to the US Navy, and they were assigned Bureau Numbers 9434–9455 and 9523–9527. The first JF-1 was delivered to the Navy in May 1934, and the US Marine Corps also acquired several. Shown here is the first Marine JF-1, BuNo 9449, assigned to Marine Utility Squadron 2 (VMJ-2).
Glenn L. Martin Maryland Aviation Museum

Bureau Number 9439 was the sixth JF-1 produced and was assigned to the utility squadron of the aircraft carrier USS *Ranger* (CV-4) in 1934. Under the rear of the fuselage is the arrestor hook for bringing the plane to a halt during carrier landings. *Tailhook Association*

A JF-1 has markings for the third plane in the 1st Section of Utility Squadron 1 (VJ-1). A navigation light in a teardrop-shaped fairing is on the tip of the upper wing. Above that wing is a small stub mast for attaching a wire antenna running from the vertical tail. *Tailhook Association*

The third JF-1, BuNo 9436, is viewed from the starboard side. The plane was painted overall in light gray, with aluminum dope on the control surfaces, including the rudder. "US NAVY" was painted in black below both of the horizontal stabilizers. *Tailhook Association*

The pilot's instrument panel in the JF-1 consisted of an upper panel and a lower panel. The black knob on the left side of the upper panel served to increase or decrease propeller RPM. At the center is the control stick, and to the left are the throttle and mixture controls. *Grumman Memorial Park*

Grumman JF-1 BuNo 9449 of VMJ-7 appears in different markings than those seen on the same plane in a preceding photo. An unusual squadron/plane-number code was used on the side of the fuselage: 703 with the letter J for Utility Squadron in the 0. *National Archives and Records Administration*

The Bureau Number on this JF-1 with markings for Marine Utility Squadron 7 (VMJ-7) appears to be 9450. A small USMC insignia appears on the fuselage below and slightly forward of the aft starboard cabane strut. An indistinct insignia is on the tail. *Naval History and Heritage Command*

JF-1 BuNo 9440 was assigned to the USS *Ranger*. The tail stripes were, front to rear, blue, white, and red, and the aircraft was painted overall light gray. The cowl on the JF-1 is called the long-chord type. The shape of the cowl would change with the J2F-1. *Grumman Memorial Park*

With its amphibious capabilities and its ability to carry a photographer and passengers, the Duck was well-suited for photographic survey work in coastal areas, and this JF-1 was employed in the Aleutian Islands Survey Expedition conducted during the 1930s. *Grumman Memorial Park*

CHAPTER 3
JF-2

The Grumman JF-2 Duck was the result of a US Coast Guard requirement for an amphibious search, rescue, and patrol aircraft. In 1934 and 1935, the Coast Guard received fourteen JF-2s, assigned USCG serial numbers 162 to 175 (170 is shown here), while the US Marine Corps acquired one JF-2, BuNo 0266. The JF-2 differed from the JF-1 in several respects, having a short-chord cowl, a Wright R-1820-102 Cyclone engine, no arrestor hook or machine gun, and a radio direction finder (RDF) loop antenna. *National Archives and Records Administration*

In addition to the Navy and the Marines, the US Coast Guard had need for an amphibian for search, rescue, and patrol work. Accordingly, the service ordered fifteen examples of the Duck. Unlike the previous Ducks, which were powered by Pratt & Whitney engines, the JF-2 sported a 750-horsepower Wright Cyclone, model R-1820-102.

The JF-2 differed from its predecessors in other ways as well, including a loop antenna-equipped radio direction finder and the lack of a tail hook.

The first JF-2, serial number 161, was transferred to the Marine Corps immediately after delivery and testing. It was then assigned Bureau Number 0266 and was attached to Quantico, Virginia-based VJ-6M. The Coast Guard aircraft, serial numbers 162 through 175, were delivered during 1934–35. On October 13, 1936, the aircraft were given new serial numbers from V135 to V148. In 1941, prior to Pearl Harbor, three Coast Guard Ducks,

V141, V144, and V146, were transferred to the US Navy, becoming Bureau Numbers 00371, 01647 and 00372.

The Coast Guard utilized the Duck to set three records—remarkably all three with the same aircraft, JF-2 167. On December 20, 1934, LCDR Elmer F. Stone set a world speed record for amphibians, with an average speed of 191.796 mph over a three-kilometer test course at Buckroe Beach, Virginia, and a top speed of 196.89 mph. On June 25, 1935, Lt. Richard L. Burke set a speed record with payload of 173.945 miles per hour over a 100-kilometer course with a 500-kilogram load. Two days later, Lt. Burke set a world record for altitude in an amphibious aircraft when he took JF-2 167 to 17,877.243 feet with a 500-kilogram load.

Beyond the Coast Guard and US Navy, the Argentine navy ordered eight duplicates of the JF-2, which Grumman supplied under their model number G-20.

The JF-2 had two prominent exhaust pipes extending below and aft of the cowl. On top of the cowl and barely visible here, but easily discerned in the preceding photograph, was the carburetor air intake. Below the aft cabane strut is the US Coast Guard insignia, and below the rear of the pilot's sliding canopy is a vertically oriented grab handle. A landing light projects from the leading edge of the bottom port wing, just inboard of the struts for the wing float. The BuNo, 170, is faintly visible on the bottom of the center float. *National Archives and Records Administration*

The profiles of the short-chord cowl and the carburetor intake of the JF-2 are easily discerned from this angle. The rudder was painted blue at the top, with red and white stripes below, and the plane's model, JF-2, was marked in white in the blue area. *National Archives and Records Administration*

US Coast Guard JF-2 BuNo 170 is observed from the aft starboard quarter. A diagonal brace was attached to the vertical fin and the horizontal stabilizer on each side. The inter-aileron struts aft of the interwing N-struts were discontinued with the J2F-1. *National Archives and Records Administration*

Although only faintly visible from this angle, US Coast Guard JF-2 BuNo 170 had "USCG" marked under each of the lower wings. The thin cross-sections of the interwing N-struts and the wing-float struts are evident when viewed from the front. *National Archives and Records Administration*

In a view from the rear of USCG JF-2 BuNo 170, the locations of the inter-aileron struts, inboard of the interwing N-struts, are visible. The tread of the main landing gear, or the distance between the bottoms of the tires, was quite narrow, at a little under eight feet. *National Archives and Records Administration*

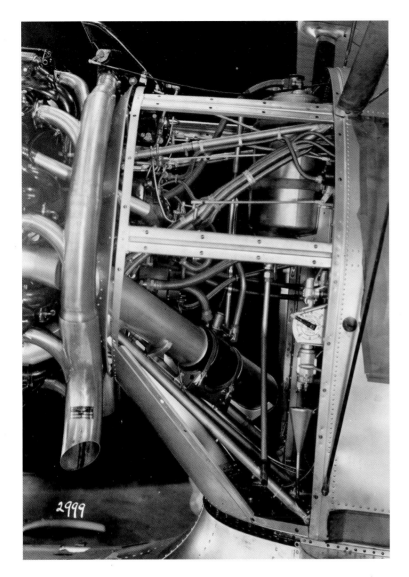

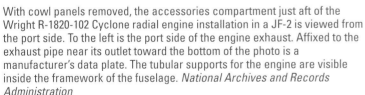

With cowl panels removed, the accessories compartment just aft of the Wright R-1820-102 Cyclone radial engine installation in a JF-2 is viewed from the port side. To the left is the port side of the engine exhaust. Affixed to the exhaust pipe near its outlet toward the bottom of the photo is a manufacturer's data plate. The tubular supports for the engine are visible inside the framework of the fuselage. *National Archives and Records Administration*

The engine accessories compartment of a Grumman JF-2 Duck is viewed from above, with the exhaust collector ring and the R-1820-102 engine to the top. The black structure above the center of the photograph is the carburetor air intake. Toward the bottom is the oil tank, with a flexible hose exiting from the top left of the tank and a rigid line exiting from the top right. A manufacturer's data plate is on the tank. *National Archives and Records Administration*

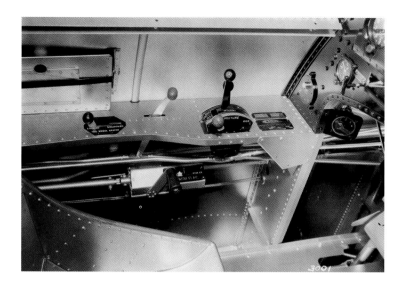

The data plate on the left console identifies this aircraft as JF-2 BuNo 170. On the console toward the left is the tail wheel locking lever, to the front of which is the throttle/mixture/spark control quadrant. Below the console is the elevator flap control. *National Archives and Records Administration*

On the pilot's instrument panel in a JF-2, at the top center is the directional gyro indicator Mk.1A. Other instruments on the upper panel include an airspeed indicator, turn and bank indicator, compass, and altitude indicator. The control stick has a contoured grip. *National Archives and Records Administration*

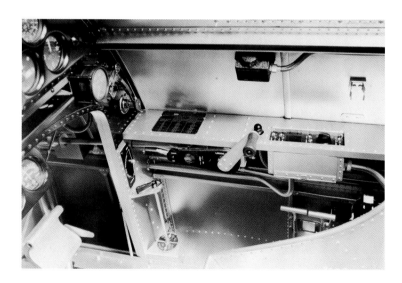

The right console of the JF-2 was spartan in layout. A fuel-gauge calibration placard is affixed to the forward part of the console, and toward the rear of the console is the main switch panel. Immediately below the console is the landing-gear operation handle. *National Archives and Records Administration*

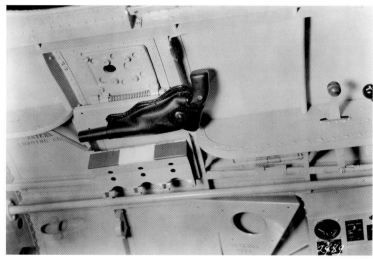

In the observer's cockpit, on the port side is a console (right) and a flare pistol in a leather case, above which is a small door for the drift sight, with a coil spring to hold it shut. The observer's cockpit contained flight controls; to the far right is the throttle control. *National Archives and Records Administration*

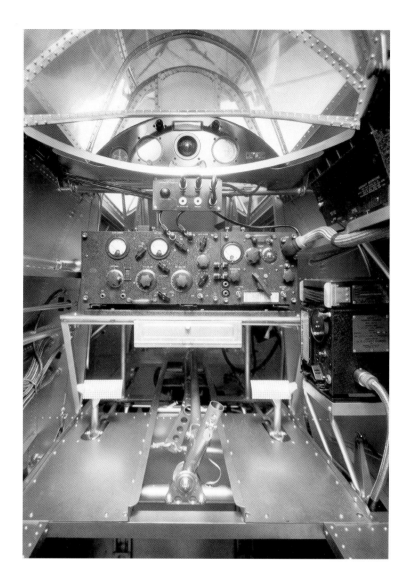
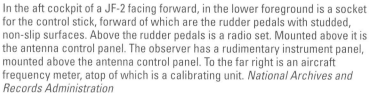

In the aft cockpit of a JF-2 facing forward, in the lower foreground is a socket for the control stick, forward of which are the rudder pedals with studded, non-slip surfaces. Above the rudder pedals is a radio set. Mounted above it is the antenna control panel. The observer has a rudimentary instrument panel, mounted above the antenna control panel. To the far right is an aircraft frequency meter, atop of which is a calibrating unit. *National Archives and Records Administration*

The main landing gear of the JF-2 (the starboard one is shown) remained virtually unchanged throughout production of the Duck. It comprised a wheel/tire assembly mounted on an axle assembly, from the top of which extended the Bendix shock strut. Also attached to the axle assembly were an upper and a lower V-shaped drag link. A hinged fairing below the lower drag link retracted when the landing gear retracted. *National Archives and Records Administration*

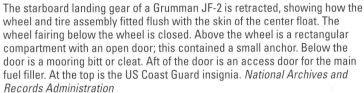

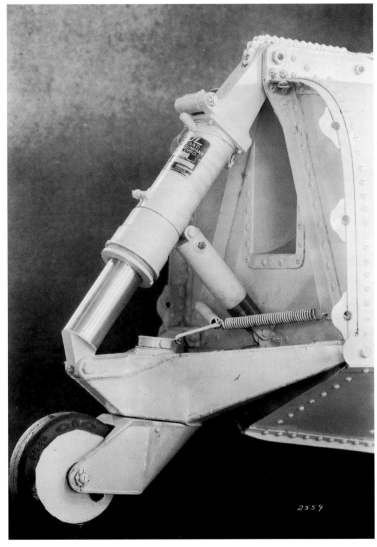

The starboard landing gear of a Grumman JF-2 is retracted, showing how the wheel and tire assembly fitted flush with the skin of the center float. The wheel fairing below the wheel is closed. Above the wheel is a rectangular compartment with an open door; this contained a small anchor. Below the door is a mooring bitt or cleat. Aft of the door is an access door for the main fuel filler. At the top is the US Coast Guard insignia. *National Archives and Records Administration*

The tail wheel of the JF-2 was mounted at the rear of the center float, or hull, of the aircraft. The wheel and tire were mounted on a caster, the top of which fitted into a link assembly that was designed to pivot on the bottom rear of the float. Extending from the rear of the link was a shock-strut assembly, the top of which rested in a pivoting mount at the upper rear of the center float. A data plate is present on the shock strut. *National Archives and Records Administration*

The starboard wing float of a JF-2 has two round inspection plugs stenciled "INSP." Near the top center of the float is another access door with a domed shape. It is secured in place with a wing nut. Two N-shaped strut assemblies hold the float to the wing. *National Archives and Records Administration*

In October 1936, the US Coast Guard changed the Bureau Numbers of its JF-2s; BuNos 162 to 175 became BuNos V135 to V148. Resting in a hangar is V139. Instead of an RDF loop antenna, a "football"-type RDF antenna has been installed on the aft deck. *Glenn L. Martin Maryland Aviation Museum*

Grumman JF-2 BuNo 173 warms its engine at Floyd Bennett Field, Brooklyn, New York. The aircraft was painted overall in a fresh-looking coat of aluminum finish, with red and white stripes under blue on the rudder. The RDF football appears to be black. *Grumman Memorial Park*

In or around 1939, a crewman, probably the observer, stands next to US Coast Guard Grumman JF-2 BuNo V136 adjacent to the administration building and control tower at Floyd Bennett Field, while in the cockpit the pilot checks the ailerons and elevators. *Grumman Memorial Park*

Displaying an aluminum finish, USCG Grumman JF-2 BuNo 162 warms its engine prior to a mission in November 1936. A thin line on the center float served to alert personnel to the position of the spinning propeller. The observer's head is visible in his cockpit. *Grumman Memorial Park*

The engine of US Coast Guard JF-2 BuNo V144 is undergoing steam-cleaning at Floyd Bennett Field in March 1940. The dark object just forward of the V144 on the fuselage is a trailing antenna fairlead, or tube, for reeling-out a wire antenna during flight. *Grumman Memorial Park*

JF Navy Bureau Numbers/Coast Guard Serial Numbers	
9218	USN XJF-1
9434-9455	USN JF-1
9523-9527	USN JF-1
439	USCG JF-1*
449	USCG JF-1**
161-175	USCG JF-2***
9835-9839	USN JF-3

* transferred from Navy, Navy BuNo 9439

** transferred from Navy, Navy BuNo 9449

*** 162-175 later reserialled V135-V174; 161 traded to US Marine Corps,
    given BuNo 0266

Grumman JF-2 BuNo V140 is being prepared for transport on a trailer. The wings, propeller, and horizontal stabilizer and elevators have been removed from the plane. The plane had an aluminum finish, with a dark anti-glare panel to the front of the cockpit. *Grumman Memorial Park*

The US Marine Corps received one JF-2, BuNo 0266, trading a Lockheed R3O-1 Electra to the Coast Guard for it in November 1935. The number 8 and "JF-2" were marked on the rudder, while the Bureau Number and an insignia were on the vertical fin. *Glenn L. Martin Maryland Aviation Museum*

CHAPTER 4
JF-3

The Navy ordered five duplicates of the JF-2, designated the JF-3. The first of these aircraft, Bureau Number 9835, was delivered on September 29, 1935, and the last, Bureau Number 9839, on October 29 of the same year. The aircraft were used to outfit Navy and Marine reserve units. Lacking tail hooks, the JF-3s were assigned to land bases, with the first and last examples being sent to Naval Air Station Anacostia, Bureau Number 9836 going to Naval Reserve Aviation Training Base Miami in Opa-locka, Florida, and 9837 and 9838 going to Naval Air Station Floyd Bennett Field, New York.

From September to October 1935, Grumman delivered five JF-3s to the US Navy and the Marine Corps Reserve. They included Bureau Numbers 9835, shown here, through 9839. They were similar to the JF-2 but were powered by the Wright R-1820-80 nine-cylinder radial engine instead of the Wright R-1820-102 of the JF-2. The JF-3 had the short-chord cowl and lacked an arrestor hook. It retained the inter-aileron struts, visible aft of the interwing N-struts, of preceding models. *National Archives and Records Administration*

Grumman JF-3 BuNo 9835 appears to have been painted in light gray. US Navy practice at this time was to paint the propeller tips with three colored bands, each four inches wide: from outside in, insignia red, light yellow, and insignia blue. *National Archives and Records Administration*

The JF-3 lacked the prominent radio direction finding loop antenna or football antenna on the turtle deck aft of the canopy, a distinguishing characteristic of the JF-2. A feature often seen on Grumman Ducks was the dark-colored non-slip area at the wing root. *National Archives and Records Administration*

The national insignia is faintly visible below the lower wing of JF-3 BuNo 9835. The JF-3s were assigned to Naval Air Stations as follows: BuNos 9835 and 9839 to Anacostia, 9836 to Opa-Locka, Florida, and BuNos 9837 and 9838 to Floyd Bennett Field. *National Archives and Records Administration*

An improved model of the Duck, with a larger float, entered production in 1936. Designated the J2F-1, the new type first flew on April 2, 1936, and was delivered to the Navy the next day. In addition to the larger float, which improved water landing characteristics, the engine model was changed from that of its predecessor. While still a Wright Cyclone, the specific model was now the R-1820-20. The J2F-1 was equipped with a tail hook, as well as a dorsal gun.

While as mentioned, the first example, Bureau Number 0162, was delivered to Naval Air Station Anacostia, in April 1936, the remainder of the type, Bureau Numbers 0163 through 0190, did not begin deliveries until January 21, 1937, with the final delivery on June 17, 1937.

During its time at Anacostia, J2F-1 BuNo 0162 was modified with full-span flaps on the upper wing. As part of this modification, the upper ailerons were deleted, and the lower ailerons lengthened.

In March 1936, the US Navy ordered an upgraded model of Duck from Grumman, designated Design 15 by Grumman and J2F by the Navy. It featured the 750-horsepower Wright R-1820-20 radial engine within a short-chord cowl similar to that of the JF-2 and the JF-3. A longer center float was employed, lengthened both at the front and to the rear, with a revised float-to-fuselage fairing toward the rear. Bureau Numbers for the first sub-model of the series, the J2F-1, were 0162 to 0190; 0188 is depicted here. *National Archives and Records Administration*

5182

With the exception of the lengthened center float, from the side the J2F-1 appeared remarkably similar to the JF-2. Improvements added to the J2F-1 included the capability to conduct photographic surveys and reconnaissance, lay smoke, and tow targets, and transport a medical patient in a stretcher. In addition, the J2F-1 also had an arrestor hook, a flexible .30-caliber machine gun mount, and provisions for underwing bomb racks. A single vertical cabane strut was added beneath the center of the upper wing. *National Archives and Records Administration*

As seen on the first Grumman J2F-1, BuNo 0162, this model of Duck retained the passenger's windows below the aft cockpit, although in an enlarged size, and now with a horizontal frame member across the window. The inter-aileron struts had been omitted. *National Archives and Records Administration*

FUSELAGE DEVELOPMENT

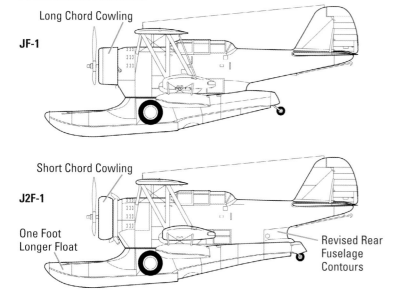

Grumman J2F-1 BuNo 0162 was assigned to NAS Anacostia and, for test purposes, was fitted with full-span flaps on the underside of the top wing instead of ailerons. The tail landing gear now had a fairing that hid most of the gear above the wheel and the caster. *National Archives and Records Administration*

Key design differences between the JF-1 and the J2F-1 are illustrated. The J2F-1 adopted the short-chord cowl of the type previously used on the JF-2 and JF-3. The center float of the J2F-1 was extended both to the front and the rear, with a revised fairing at the rear.

Viewed from the front, the J2F-1 looked strikingly similar to the preceding Grumman Ducks with short-chord cowls. Visible on the leading edge of the port wing forward of the national insignia is the landing light. The main wheels were slightly canted. *National Archives and Records Administration*

A J2F-1 is observed from aft. The X-shaped rigging between the upper and the lower wings was referred to as rigging tie rods. These were not flying wires *per se*, but rather thin, streamlined steel strips designed to add reinforcement to the wings. *National Archives and Records Administration*

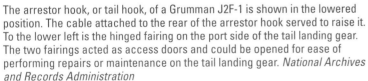

The arrestor hook, or tail hook, of a Grumman J2F-1 is shown in the lowered position. The cable attached to the rear of the arrestor hook served to raise it. To the lower left is the hinged fairing on the port side of the tail landing gear. The two fairings acted as access doors and could be opened for ease of performing repairs or maintenance on the tail landing gear. *National Archives and Records Administration*

The main landing gear of the J2F-1 was the same design as used in earlier versions of the Grumman Duck. This port landing gear includes a smooth-tread tire. Extending diagonally from the top of the axle assembly to the upper part of the landing gear bay is the Bendix shock strut. The tubular object on the side of the upper part of the shock strut is a counterbalance. *National Archives and Records Administration*

The fairings on the sides of the tail landing gear of a J2F-1 are shown in the open position, showing the hinges and coil springs that are included in the fairing assemblies. A manufacturer's plate headed "Bendix Pneumatic Shock" is affixed to the strut. *National Archives and Records Administration*

Attached to four mounts under the wing, the bomb rack was fabricated from two T-profile frame members, atop which were cross-members for the bomb shackles. The objects shaped like inverted Ys on the bottom of the front cross-member are sway braces. *National Archives and Records Administration*

The port wing float of a J2F-1 is exhibited. It was mounted on two sets of struts forming the shape of the letter N when viewed from the front or rear. Two tie rods forming an X shape were attached to the inboard sides of these struts. *National Archives and Records Administration*

Five fragmentation bombs are shackled to the port underwing bomb rack of a J2F-1. The sway braces acted to prevent the bombs from shifting around on the bomb rack. The upper fin of the closest bomb is secured to a clip on the rear cross-member of the rack. *National Archives and Records Administration*

An engine installation on a J2F-1 is viewed from overhead. The cowl is still installed around the engine. The dark object jutting out over the top of the cowl is the carburetor air intake, a curved, dark-colored scoop with its opening pointing forward. Aft of the cowl is the collector ring for the exhaust. Farther aft is the oil tank. Elements of the frame to which the removable panels of the engine accessory compartment are attached are also visible. *National Archives and Records Administration*

The pilot's cockpit of a Grumman J2F-1 Duck is observed from above, with the windscreen to the top of the photo and the pilot's seat at the center. Instead of a solid floorboard, the cockpit was equipped with channel-type foot rests, between which is the control stick. As in preceding models of the Grumman Duck, the pilot's instrument panel comprised an upper and a lower panel, with a retractable, sliding chart table between the panels. *National Archives and Records Administration*

In a view of the pilot's seat and left console, the wheel-shaped object situated vertically in the console is the rudder trim-tab control, below which is the elevator flap control. The lever aft of the throttle/mixture/spark quadrant is the wobble-pump handle. *National Archives and Records Administration*

The rear cockpit is viewed facing forward. The two small instrument panels contain a clock, altimeter, compass, and airspeed indicator. Between the panels is the back of the pilot's headrest. Below the panels is a locker for storing secret and confidential documents. *National Archives and Records Administration*

On the right console of the J2F-1 is the manufacturer's data plate and a fuel-gauge calibration placard, with the main switch panel toward the rear of the console. The vertical black handle toward the upper right was the cockpit closure control. *National Archives and Records Administration*

There was a recess in the turtle deck of the fuselage in which the ammunition box holder of the flexible .30-caliber machine gun rested when the gun was stowed. The gun was mounted on a truck which could be moved on the race, or track, inside the cockpit. *National Archives and Records Administration*

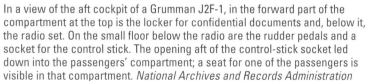

In a view of the aft cockpit of a Grumman J2F-1, in the forward part of the compartment at the top is the locker for confidential documents and, below it, the radio set. On the small floor below the radio are the rudder pedals and a socket for the control stick. The opening aft of the control-stick socket led down into the passengers' compartment; a seat for one of the passengers is visible in that compartment. *National Archives and Records Administration*

Located aft of the radio operator's compartment are parachute flare containers, the two large canted tubes visible here. At bottom, the rods and cables that actuate the control surfaces of the J2F-1 are clearly visible inside the aircraft. *National Archives and Records Administration*

The photographer probably stood in the hatch to the passengers' compartment to take this view of the aft cockpit facing forward in a J2F-1. In the left foreground is the control-stick socket; the control stick is stowed on the bulkhead at the center of the photo. *National Archives and Records Administration*

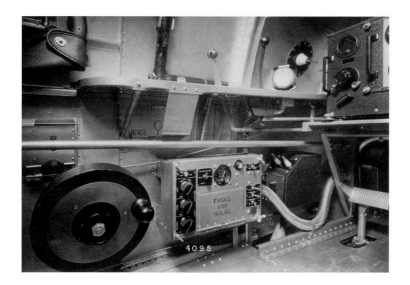

In a view of the lower port side of the aft cockpit, to the left is the reel for a trailing antenna. Forward of the reel is an electrical distribution panel with a compartment for fuses and bulbs at its center. The left rudder pedal is to the lower right, below the radio. *National Archives and Records Administration*

Since the Grumman Duck was part watercraft, it required an anchor. A door hinged on the forward edge and fitted with two thumbscrew-type locks covered a small compartment for an anchor on the starboard side of the fuselage above the landing-gear bay. Part of the anchor and its rope cable are visible inside the opening. Also visible is the lower part of the auxiliary fuel tank. *National Archives and Records Administration*

In the 1930s, floatplanes and amphibious aircraft such as the Grumman Duck often operated from US Navy aircraft carriers. Here, crewmen are pushing J2F-1 BuNo 0170 of the utility unit of USS *Yorktown* (CV-5) on the hangar deck in October 1937. *National Museum of Naval Aviation*

Grumman J2F-1 BuNo 0169 of USS *Yorktown*'s utility unit is on that carrier's number-two elevator on November 2, 1937. The black stripe on the lower wing parallel to the leading edge apparently indicated a permissible walkway along the wing. *Naval History and Heritage Command*

Three J2F-1s assigned to Fleet Air Base Pearl Harbor fly abreast in formation over farmlands around the late 1930s. Their fuselage markings include individual aircraft numbers, separated from "FLEET AIR BASE" with a dash: they are 10, 8, and 9. *National Museum of Naval Aviation*

The same three Grumman J2F-1 Ducks shown in the preceding photo are viewed from the port side. Although difficult to see in the photo, "US NAVY" is marked under the horizontal stabilizers in letters as large as those in "FLEET AIR BASE." *National Museum of Naval Aviation*

The number nine plane of Fleet Air Base Pearl Harbor, the J2F-1 to the right in the preceding photo, was BuNo 0189, and the photo was dated November 15, 1939. This plane was lost while based at Dutch Harbor, Alaska Territory, in July 1943. *National Museum of Naval Aviation*

Grumman J2F-1 BuNo 0162, assigned to Naval Air Station Anacostia, flies a mission on December 4, 1938. The plane lacked unit markings; visible markings include the Bureau Number and model type on the tail and "US NAVY" under the horizontal stabilizer. *National Museum of Naval Aviation*

A J2F-1 assigned to the utility unit of USS *Saratoga* (CV-3) taxis on a runway, most likely at San Diego, California, around 1941. The plane was painted overall in light gray and has a national insignia and "USS SARATOGA–5" in white on the fuselage. *Naval History and Heritage Command*

Marine Utility Squadron 1 (VMJ-1) flew Grumman J2F-1 BuNo 0186 in the late 1930s. It seems to have had an aluminum finish, with red, white, and blue rudder stripes. In June 1939, VMJ-1 had in its inventory one Grumman JF-1, one JF-2, and one J2F-1. *Glenn L. Martin Maryland Aviation Museum*

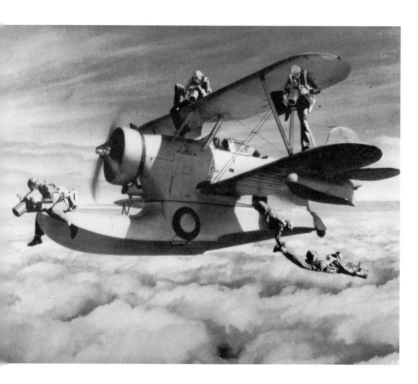

No, these are not real photographers poised dangerously on a J2F-1 in flight; rather, this is a composite photo of a plane with VJ-2's insignia, poking fun at Grumman Duck reconnaissance photographers' efforts to achieve the best camera angles during missions. *Naval History and Heritage Command*

In this vintage color photograph, a US Coast Guard J2F-1 warms its engine prior to a mission. Grumman J2F-1s also served with the US Navy and the US Marine Corps. Worthy of notice are the red propeller warning stripe on the center float and the manner in which the orange-yellow color of the top of the upper wing continues under the leading edge of the wing. *Stan Piet collection*

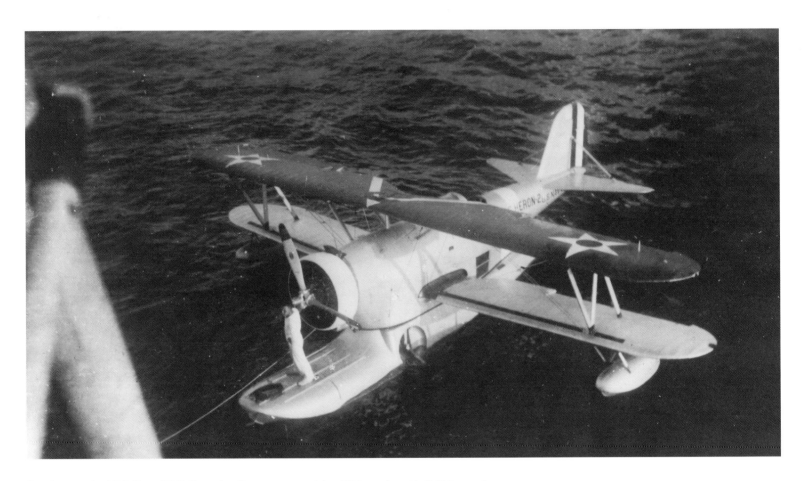

Seaplane tender USS *Heron* (AVP-2) sends a line out to one of the J2F-1s assigned to it. This seaplane tender, formerly a minesweeper, served with the Asiatic Fleet in the Far East through the 1930s, during which time several Grumman Ducks were attached to her. *National Museum of Naval Aviation*

Grumman J2F-1 BuNo 0181 at NAS Guantánamo Bay, Cuba, in May 1942, was painted light gray, with red and white rudder stripes and a national insignia with a red circle in the middle on the fuselage. "NAS Guantanamo Bay" is marked forward of the insignia. *National Museum of Naval Aviation*

The same J2F-1, BuNo 0181, seen in the preceding photo is viewed from another angle with a crewman wearing a parachute and harness posing alongside it. Silhouetted against the forward end of the center float is a general-purpose bomb on the underwing rack. *National Museum of Naval Aviation*

CHAPTER 6
J2F-2

The next version of the Duck was also built for the Navy, featuring a slightly more powerful engine (790 horsepower vs. 750 horsepower), the Wright R-1820-30. Thirty examples of the new model, designated J2F-2, were delivered between June 6, and November 18, 1938. Thirteen of these were furnished to the Marines at Quantico and Norfolk, with the remainder going to the Navy, two to Cavite, Philippines and the balance to Anacostia. The aircraft bore Bureau Numbers 0780 through 0794, and 1195 through 1209.

The first J2F-2, BuNo 0780, exhibits a factory-fresh paint job and basic markings: national insignia under the lower wings, "US NAVY" under the horizontal stabilizer, and the Bureau Number and model on the vertical tail. Red, yellow, and blue stripes are on the tips and outer parts of the propeller blades. *National Archives and Records Administration*

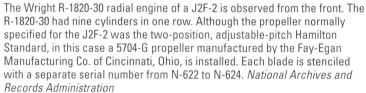

The Wright R-1820-30 radial engine of a J2F-2 is observed from the front. The R-1820-30 had nine cylinders in one row. Although the propeller normally specified for the J2F-2 was the two-position, adjustable-pitch Hamilton Standard, in this case a 5704-G propeller manufactured by the Fay-Egan Manufacturing Co. of Cincinnati, Ohio, is installed. Each blade is stenciled with a separate serial number from N-622 to N-624. *National Archives and Records Administration*

Little documentation has been found concerning this fixed machine gun mounting in a J2F-2. Some believe this to be characteristic of the J2F-2A sub-variant. The fixed Browning .30-caliber machine gun is mounted above the engine accessory compartment, toward the upper center of the photo. The barrel of the machine gun protruded through a gap between two of the cylinders of the engine. An interrupter gear prevented the machine gun from firing when a propeller blade was directly in front of the gun. *National Archives and Records Administration*

In the pilot's cockpit of a J2F-2, the light-colored object to the far left was a small spotlight. A checklist for takeoff and landing on land is on the fairing to left of the instrument panel, and one for takeoffs and landings on water is on the right fairing. *National Archives and Records Administration*

A J2F-2 of VJ-1 at Naval Auxiliary Air Station Corry Field, Florida, in 1938 displays the number 24 on the lower wing. Between the cabane struts is the squadron's insignia: a pelican carrying a mail bag, with a photographer's mate clutched securely in its beak. *National Museum of Naval Aviation*

Aircraft number 19 of VJ-1 was J2F-2 BuNo 0789. The observer is waving to the photographer, and a passenger is visible through the window below the aft cockpit. The horizontal tail and vertical tail and the strut between them were painted Willow Green. *Naval History and Heritage Command*

CHAPTER 7

J2F-2A

The last nine J2F-2 Ducks, Bureau Numbers 1198 though 1209, were modified for the Marine Corps, becoming J2F-2As in 1939. These aircraft were assigned to VMS-3 for duty in the Caribbean, serving as Neutrality Patrol.

For this service they were equipped with twin .30-caliber machine guns, rather than a single mount, and could carry 250-pound depth bombs. The aircraft operated from Marine Corps Air Field St. Thomas (Bourne Field), which was redesignated Marine Corps Air Station St. Thomas on December 1, 1941. By that time, the squadron was operating seven of the J2F-2As. While VMS-3's Ducks never attacked a U-boat, it could be argued that they were somewhat effective, as the German submarines stayed outside of the Grumman's range.

By the end of 1942 the Squadron's J2F-2As had largely been replaced by OS2N-1 Kingfishers, and the Ducks relegated to less demanding uses.

Crewmen of a J2F-2A assigned to the Fleet Air Photographic Squadron, Atlantic is used in the staged rescue of a downed aviator at sea at Norfolk in 1943. Nine J2F-2s were converted to J2F-2As, BuNos 1198–1206, for the US Marine Corps by substituting a twin flexible .30-caliber machine gun mount for the single flexible .30-caliber mount, and including provisions for installing wing racks for depth bombs. These planes originally flew with VMS-3 in the Caribbean conducting Neutrality Patrols. *National Archives and Records Administration*

In 1940, J2F-2As of VMS-3 based at St. Thomas, Virgin Islands, conduct a Neutrality Patrol to monitor the movements of warring parties in the Western Hemisphere. The large national insignia on the forward fuselage was devised especially for these patrols. *National Museum of Naval Aviation*

Six Grumman J2F-2As of Marine Scouting Squadron 3 (VMS-3) conduct a Neutrality Patrol mission over the Caribbean around 1941. This squadron received its J2F-2As in 1939. A bomb rack is faintly visible below the lower starboard wing of the closest plane. *National Museum of Naval Aviation*

JF/J2F Data

	JF-1	JF-2	JF-3	J2F-1	J2F-2	J2F-3	J2F-4	J2F-5	J2F-6
Engine	P&W	Wright	Wright	Wright	Wright	Wright	Wright	Wright	Wright
Engine model	R-1830-62	R-1820-102	R-1820-80	R-1820-20	R-1820-30	R-1820-30	R-1820-30	R-1820-50	R-1820-54
Armament	1 x .30-cal. 200 lbs. bombs	None	None	1 x .30-cal. 200 lbs. bombs	1 x .30-cal. 200 lbs. bombs	None	1 x .30-cal. 500 lbs. bombs	1 x .30-cal.	1 x .30-cal. 650 lbs. bombs
Wingspan	39´	39´	39´	39´	39´	39´	39´	39´	39´
Length	33´	33´	33´	34´	34´	34´	34´	34´	34´
Height	14´6˝	14´6˝	14´6˝	14´6˝	14´6˝	14´6˝	14´6˝	14´6˝	14´6˝
Empty Weight	4,133 lbs						4,300 lbs	5,480 lbs	
Max Weight	5,375 lbs							6,711 lbs	7,325 lbs
Max Speed	168 mph						190 mph	188 mph	190 mph
Normal Range (mi)								780	875
Service ceiling (ft)	18,000	18,000	18,000					27,000	25,750

Built in 1939, the next version of the Duck was the unarmed J2F-3, which was primarily used as a VIP transport. Twenty examples were delivered between February 1, 1939 and June 26, 1939. These aircraft bore the Bureau Numbers 1568 through 1587.

Mechanically, the aircraft essentially duplicated the J2F-2 except the new model included a Hamilton Standard constant-speed propeller. Some sources indicate that these aircraft were fitted with plush interiors, but this has yet to be confirmed.

Grumman delivered twenty J2F-3s in 1939, Bureau Numbers 1568 to 1587. These essentially were J2F-2s shorn of their machine guns and fitted with Wright R-1820-36 engines driving Hamilton Standard constant-speed propellers. The J2F-3s were used as transports for VIPs such as admirals and US Naval attachés. RADM William Brown, commandant of the US Naval Academy, was assigned one, BuNo 1569, shown here. The USNA insignia is between the cabane struts, and two stars representing a rear admiral are affixed to the fuselage aft of the rear cockpit. *National Archives and Records Administration*

RADM Brown's J2F-3 is viewed from another angle. Thin stripes were applied along the waterline of the center float and also on the wing floats. The Hamilton Standard constant-speed propeller was distinguished by the cylindrical hub extension. *National Archives and Records Administration*

The J2F-3 assigned to RADM Brown, although lacking machine guns, still had bomb racks underneath the lower wings. The forward ends of the light-colored lines along the center float ended at the chine, and the float had a light-colored nose. *National Archives and Records Administration*

Brown's J2F-3 exhibited the Class 1 scheme for painting USN admirals' aircraft: Admiral Blue fuselage and floats, aluminum wings and vertical and horizontal tails, except orange-yellow on top of the upper wing. All paint was buffed to a high gloss. *National Archives and Records Administration*

The J2F-3 assigned to RADM Brown was delivered to the US Naval Academy in February 1939. It had the red, yellow, and blue stripes on the propeller that were typical of that era. Oval-shaped Hamilton Standard logos are applied to the propeller blades. *National Archives and Records Administration*

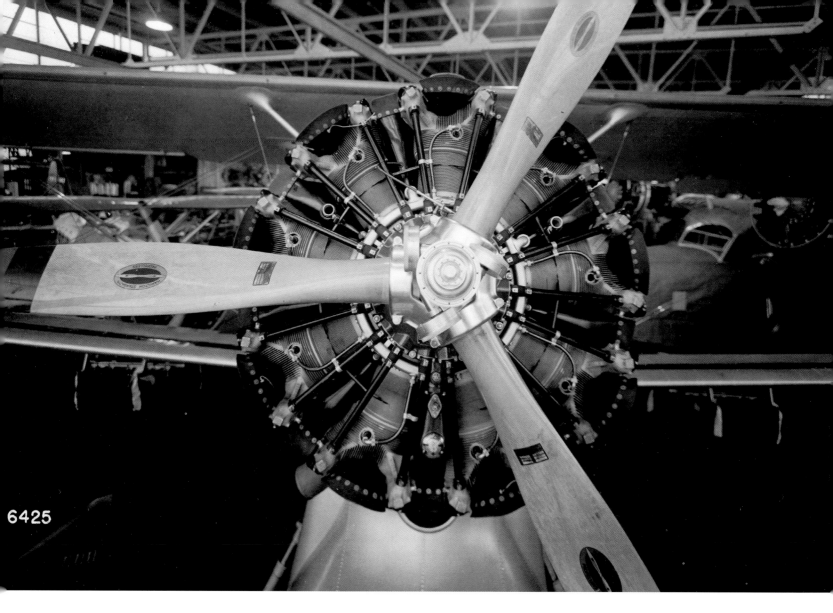

6425

The cowl of a J2F-3 has been removed, allowing a clear frontal view of the Wright R-1820-36 radial engine. On each of the propeller blades is a decal with the Hamilton Standard logo and a plate giving the propeller's drawing number and other data. *National Archives and Records Administration*

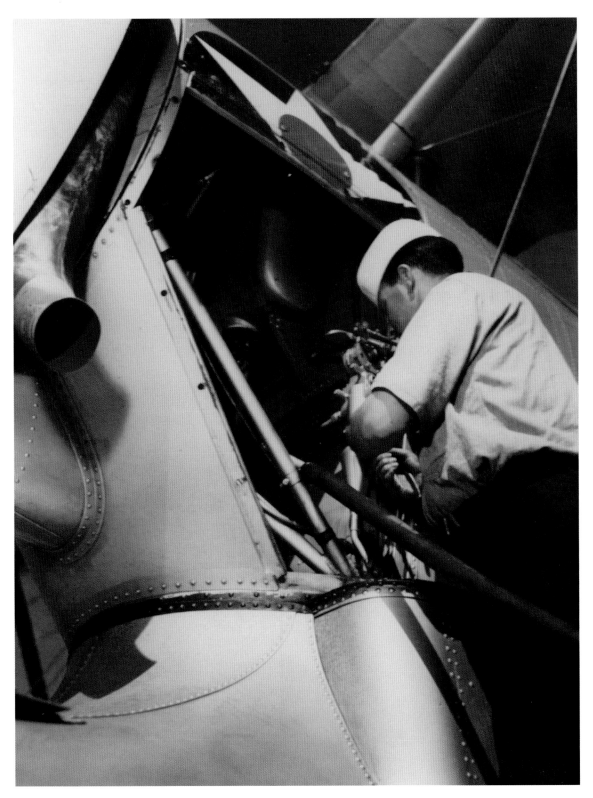

An aviation mechanic performs repairs on a J2F-3 assigned to VJ-4 around 1940. A cover on the port side of the engine-accessory compartment has been removed, and part of the engine exhaust and the Neutrality Patrol national insignia are in view. The orange-yellow of the top of the upper wing wraps around the leading edge of the wing; this feature was instituted when it was found that it allowed for smoother airflow over the leading edge. *Naval History and Heritage Command*

Two J2F-3s fly over Molokai, Hawaii Territory, in 1940. On BuNo 1577 (foreground), a broad, black band was painted along the side of the center float at the waterline, and the squadron insignia of VJ-1 was applied to the fuselage between the cabane struts. *National Museum of Naval Aviation*

To the right, a line of Grumman J2F-3s face a line of Grumman Martlet IIs, the Fleet Air Arm's version of the F4F-3 Wildcat. All of the J2F-3s have the Neutrality Patrol national insignia on the forward part of the fuselage, and fabric covers are over the cowls. *Grumman Memorial Park*

Grumman J2F-3 BuNo 1578 was delivered to NAS Jacksonville, Florida, in mid-January 1940, and displays the prewar national insignia with a red circle in the center of the star. Part of the "NAVAL AIR STATION" inscription on the fuselage is discernible. *Tailhook Association*

Civilians inspect Grumman J2F-3 BuNo 1570 assigned to Naval Air Station Jacksonville. The letter J is between the lines of the NAS Jacksonville markings on the side of the fuselage. A bomb rack is visible under the wing and above the wing float. *Tailhook Association*

A boom on the *Omaha*-class light cruiser *Concord* (CL-10) is being used to position a J2F-3 in waters off Hanga Roa, Easter Island, on November 10, 1943. Written in script on the forward part of the fuselage is the plane's nickname, *The Galloping Ghost*. *Naval History and Heritage Command*

The fourth J2F-3, BuNo 1571, flies over a coastline around 1939. In addition to serving as VIP aircraft, J2F-3s also operated with utility units on various aircraft carriers and at Naval Air Stations. The US Naval Mission at Rio de Janeiro had a J2F-3 in late 1941. *National Museum of Naval Aviation*

In 1939, J2F-3 BuNo 1571, based at Naval Air Station Minneapolis, Minnesota, flies above Midwestern farmlands. The aircraft was painted overall in aluminum. Jutting from the fuselage just aft of the aft cockpit is the fairlead and weight for the trailing antenna. *National Museum of Naval Aviation*

A two-color camouflage scheme of Non-Specular (NS) blue-gray over NS light gray is present on this J2F-3 with landing gear extended. The national insignia is of the type authorized from May 1942 to June 1943, with the red circle removed from the star. *National Museum of Naval Aviation*

From September 1939, through June 1940, the Navy took delivery of thirty-two J2F-4 aircraft. These aircraft, largely duplicates of the earlier J2F-2, were the last of the series to be powered by the 790-horsepower Wright R-1820-20. The J2F-4s differed from the previous model with slight variations in towing equipment, smoke dischargers, and armament. The Navy assigned Bureau Numbers 1639 through 1670 to this group of aircraft. Four virtually identical aircraft were produced for sale to Argentina under the Grumman model number G-15. They were delivered in November 1939.

The J2F-4 model of Grumman Duck was delivered from September 1939 to June 1940, and encompassed Bureau Numbers 1639 to 1670. They were similar to the Grumman J2F-3 but were equipped with machine guns and the capability to mount smoke-laying and target-towing apparatuses. The J2F-4s also had minor differences in their flight instruments and engine functions. The first J2F-4, BuNo 1639, is depicted. It was finished overall in aluminum with a black band along the center float. *National Archives and Records Administration*

Two beaching crewmen manhandle the wing floats of the first J2F-4, BuNo 1639, on November 6, 1939. A good view is available of the waterline with reference to the center float. Between the mufflers below the cowl is the oil-cooler air intake scoop. *National Museum of Naval Aviation*

In a view of a J2F-4 from aft, the model of the plane is marked in black on the rudder. The black band at the waterline of the float is faintly visible. Trim tabs are present at the lower trailing edge of the rudder and toward the inboard sides of the elevators. *National Museum of Naval Aviation*

The pilot of Grumman J2F-4 BuNo 1655 assigned to NAS Pensacola, Florida, walks away to the left as ground crewmen secure the plane. The national insignia on the orange-yellow top wing were of the prewar type, with red circles inside the white stars. *National Museum of Naval Aviation*

J2F-2 BuNo 1669 suffered an accident from a sheared landing-gear pin at NAS Guantánamo Bay on March 1, 1943. The device shaped like an electric fan next to the foot of the man to the right was the impeller that powered the target-towing equipment. *National Museum of Naval Aviation*

A large Neutrality Patrol national insignia is prominent on the forward part of the fuselage of a J2F-4 assigned to VJ-4 around 1940. The vertical and horizontal tails were painted insignia red. A band was painted around the fuselage aft of the rear cockpit. *National Museum of Naval Aviation*

The number-24 plane of Utility Squadron 3 cuts a fine profile as it soars above the clouds in or around 1940. The three colored bands on the outer part of the propeller blades are visible in the blur created by the spinning props. In June 1940, two Grumman J2F-4s were assigned to VJ-3, but by November 31, 1941, only one J2F-4 was listed in the inventory of Utility Squadron 3's aircraft. *National Museum of Naval Aviation*

Three J2F-4s attached to VJ-2's Hawaii Detachment and a solitary PBY Catalina at NAS Ford Island stand witness to the Japanese attack on Pearl Harbor on December 7, 1941. Fabric covers are fitted over the Ducks' cockpit canopies. The tails were lemon yellow. *National Museum of Naval Aviation*

A small number of Grumman Ducks survive, including this beautifully restored Grumman J2F-4, BuNo 1649, currently civil registration number NL63850. As of this writing, it was owned by Amphib, Inc., of Lake Zurich, Illinois. This aircraft was serving with Utility Squadron 1 (VJ-1) at NAS Ford Island at the time of the December 7, 1941 attack and survived the Japanese air strikes. After serving through the rest of the war, the plane was sold as war surplus to a Bahamian firm. Bureau Number 1649 crashed into a lake in the Bahamas in 1955, but was salvaged in the 1990s. *Rich Kolasa*

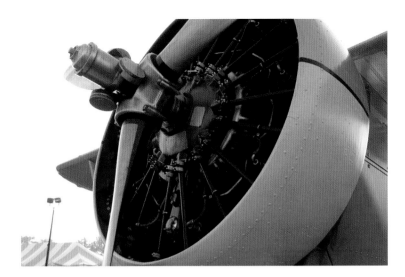

Grumman J2F-4 BuNo 1649 is equipped with a Hamilton Standard constant-speed propeller. The cowl is of riveted construction. Within it is a Wright Cyclone engine. The original engine on the J2F-4 was the 790-horsepower Wright R-1820-36 Cyclone radial engine. *David Doyle*

The cowl is viewed from the port side. Aft of the cowl is the exhaust collector ring and, protruding below the cowl, the port-side exhaust tail pipe. (A tin can is wired to the exhaust to collect dripping oil.) The boxy object to the upper rear of the cowl is the carburetor air intake. To the right is the engine-accessory compartment, with removable covers. *David Doyle*

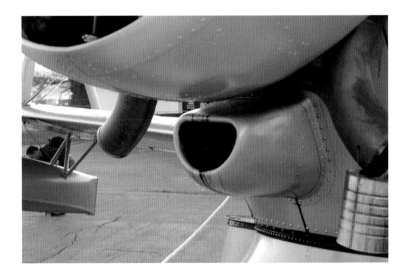

The oil-cooler intake scoop below and aft of the cowl appears to have been a modification of the original configuration of the intake. A December 1946 photograph of the same aircraft shows that an air scoop was present in this location by that time. *David Doyle*

The removable panels of the engine-accessories compartment are secured in place with slotted round-headed screws. Three louvers are incorporated into each of these panels for ventilation. To the upper right is the insignia of Utility Squadron 1 (VJ-1). *David Doyle*

As seen facing forward and to the starboard, fastened to the top of the center float are T-channels for stiffening. On the top center of the float are two oval panels with round inspection plugs in them, stenciled "INSP" and fastened in place with thumbscrews. *David Doyle*

The forward part of the joint between the center float of the J2F-4 and the fuselage is viewed from the port side, with the port main landing gear bay to the lower right. The top of the float has a pronounced ledge, painted black on this example, in this spot. *David Doyle*

The forward inspection plug is shown. To the front top of the float is a mooring cable or anchor cable holder. It has two overlapping tongs on top of it, making it easy to insert the cable into it. Once the cable was seated in the holder, the tongs acted to hold it in place. *David Doyle*

Grumman J2F-4 BuNo 1649 has been restored in its original colors and markings for Utility Squadron 1. The finish is aluminum, with orange-yellow upper wing top and cowl bottom, willow green vertical and horizontal tails, and black squadron/aircraft-number markings. *Rich Kolasa*

On the fuselage between the cabane struts, which help support the upper wing, is the squadron insignia for Utility Squadron 1. The insignia features a flying pelican with a photographer's mate nestled in its beak and a mail bag clutched in its feet. *David Doyle*

The N-struts acted to hold the upper and lower wings together and to add rigidity to the wings. Seen here are the attachment points of the port N-struts to the underside of the upper wing, as well as the interplane rigging tie rods to the lower left of the photo. *David Doyle*

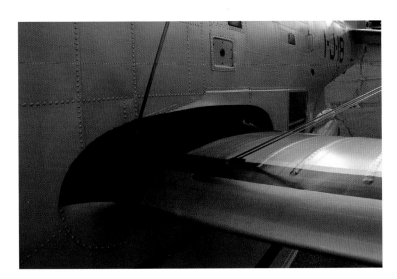

The lower port wing root is observed from the leading edge. The fillet between the wing root and the fuselage was commonly painted black on Grumman Ducks. The recessed panel at the upper center is where the target-towing impeller was attached. *David Doyle*

The lower attachment points of the port N-struts are illustrated. A streamlined interplane tie rod spacer (top left) acted to keep the tie rods in their proper place. Jutting out from the leading edge of the wing inboard of the N-struts is the landing light. *David Doyle*

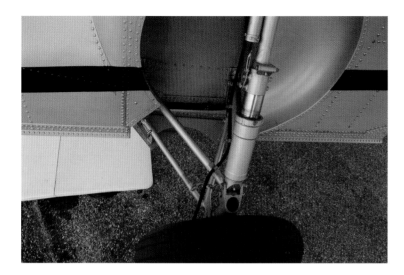

The port landing gear is viewed, with the landing gear bay to the top and the tire at the bottom, next to which is the upper part of the hollow axle assembly, which has two V-shaped drag links attached to its sides. Attached to the top of the axle assembly is the shock strut. *David Doyle*

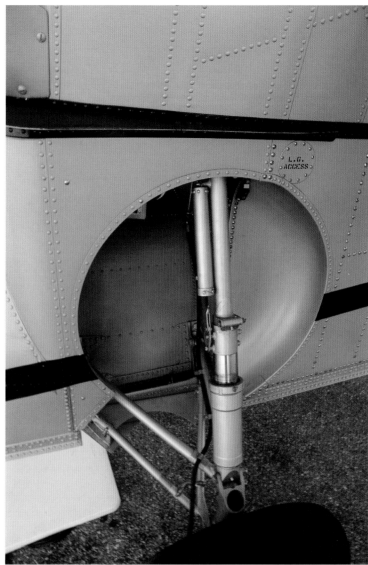

The shock strut extends to the top of the landing gear bay. The cylinder on the forward (left in the photo) side of the upper part of the strut is a counterbalance. On the fuselage skin to the upper aft edge of the landing gear bay is a small, round access plate for the landing gear; it is stenciled "LG ACCESS." The black stripe on the side of the center float, forward and aft of the landing gear bay, marked the waterline of the plane when it was in the water. *David Doyle*

The port tire (left), axle assembly, and drag links are viewed from aft facing forward. At the center is the fairing for the lower part of the landing gear. Details of the locking nuts that secure the drag links and the shock strut to the axle assembly are also visible. *David Doyle*

The pilot's sliding canopy is open in this view of Grumman J2F-4 BuNo 1649, but the rear cockpit canopy is closed. The angle of the black band indicating the waterline on the side of the center float is apparent. The national insignia are the prewar type with the red circles. *Rich Kolasa*

Centered on the top wing is a forward-pointing chevron of a slightly different shade of yellow than the surrounding orange-yellow wingtop. The chevron has a thin black border. The color on the tail replicates VJ-1's squadron color, willow green. *Rich Kolasa*

On each side of the empennage is a diagonal strut between the vertical fin and the horizontal stabilizer. The elevator is in the raised position, and on its inboard side is the elevator trim tab. The red cord and wooden piece to the left make up a rudder lock. *David Doyle*

The fairings over the tail landing gear at the rear end of the center float are hinged on their forward edges to allow easy access to the landing gear. A fixed fairing extends from the top rear of the float. The wheel and its caster are rotated 180 degrees to the rear. *David Doyle*

The raised starboard elevator is viewed from over the horizontal stabilizer. The elevator and vertical fin had aluminum frames covered with fabric skin, while the horizontal stabilizer as well as the rudder had aluminum frames and aluminum-alloy skin. *David Doyle*

The port wing float is suspended below the wing by two tubular N-struts, with X-shaped rigging wires on the inboard side of the struts adding rigidity to the assembly. The float is of riveted aluminum-alloy construction. A small data plate is riveted to the top of it. *David Doyle*

The pilot's sliding section of canopy pushed back over the fixed center section of the canopy. The two sliding sections over the aft cockpit remain in the closed position. Two vertical grab handles are present on the side of the fuselage below the aft-cockpit canopy. *Rich Kolasa*

To the front of the windscreen on the top deck of the fuselage is a single, vertical cabane strut attached to the center of the upper wing. This strut was added starting with the J2F-1. Two handholds, painted black, are built into the trailing edge of the upper wing. *David Doyle*

On the fuselage above the starboard passenger's window are three recessed steps and two vertical grab handles, to assist crewmen in climbing up to the cockpits. A small step is also built into the upper part of the center float below the passenger's window. *David Doyle*

Fairings are employed on the joints between the cabane struts and the bottom of the upper wing. Smaller fairings are on the joints between the bottoms of the cabane struts and the fuselage. Also present are criss-crossing tie rods and the VJ-1 squadron insignia. *David Doyle*

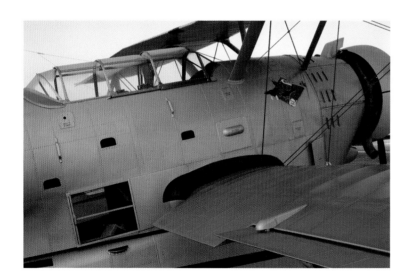

Below the canopy to the upper left is a small door for deploying the drift meter, an instrument that enabled the observer to calculate the amount of drift of the aircraft from its intended course. The panel with the bulge above the wing is the battery cover. *David Doyle*

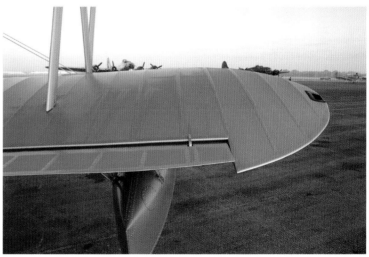

The aileron on the lower starboard wing is shown, including the outboard hinge and the cutout in the leading edge of the aileron to provide clearance for the hinge. On the tip of the wing is a built-in hand hold, grasped by ground crewmen when moving the plane. *David Doyle*

The Grumman Duck's wing floats, such as this starboard one, were fabricated from aluminum sections, riveted together, with reinforcing strips where necessary. The N-struts that hold the float to the wing are attached to angle-brackets riveted to the float. *David Doyle*

On the tip of the upper wing is a navigation light with a green lens housed in a teardrop-shaped fairing. The aileron is visible on the rear of the upper wing; slots for hinges are on the leading edge of the aileron. The wings were formed from aluminum frames with doped fabric stretched over them. This made for a lightweight structure, but one subject to rips and other damage. Maintenance crewmen were adept at repairing the fabric. *David Doyle*

The starboard wing float and the lower starboard wing tip with its handhold are viewed from another angle. U-shaped fittings on the bottoms of the struts that hold the float to the wing are attached with screws and nuts to the angle-brackets on the float. *David Doyle*

Grumman J2F-4 BuNo 1649 cuts a stunning figure, restored to its 1941 appearance. This aircraft is a significant historical artifact, having survived the December 7, 1941 attack on Pearl Harbor. Amazingly, this Duck was still flying some seventy years after the "Day of Infamy." *Rich Kolasa*

CHAPTER 10

J2F-5

Seeking to improve performance, the next model of the Duck, as the aircraft had become officially designated during J2F-5 production, was powered by the Wright R-1820-50 Cyclone, which developed 950 horsepower—about a twenty-percent increase over that of the R-1820-20 used by the earlier J2F-4. The new engine required a deeper cowl, making the J2F-5 visibly and immediately distinguishable from earlier models.

Taking advantage of the extra power available, and in view of the worldwide situation, the wings of the J2F-5 were strengthened in order to support improved bomb racks, allowing the transport and release of 325-pound depth charges.

The J2F-5 would be the Duck variant produced in the largest quantity by Grumman, with 144 examples being delivered between July 1941, and March 1942. The aircraft were assigned Bureau Numbers 00659 through 00802.

The Grumman J2F-5 brought a number of changes to the Duck compared to the J2F-4. The 950-horsepower Wright R-1820-50 Cyclone engine was adopted, and covering it was a newly designed long-chord cowl, virtually cylindrical in shape, with a rolled front edge. The frames of the wings near the bomb racks were reinforced to enable the plane to deliver two 325-pound depth charges. Grumman delivered the first J2F-5s to the Navy in July 1941, and a total of 144 were produced, Bureau Numbers 00659 to 00802. The J2F-5 in this photo was the first of the -5 model. *National Archives and Records Administration*

In the aft cockpit of the first J2F-5 was a single flexible Browning .30-caliber machine gun. A small bomb, probably a 100-pound general-purpose type, is on the wing rack. Each passenger's window retained the single horizontal frame member across the center. *National Archives and Records Administration*

No markings were visible on the first J2F-5, BuNo 00659, including the model and the Bureau Number that should be on the vertical tail. The carburetor air intake juts out above the upper rear of the cowl. A red navigation light was present on the tip of the upper wing. *National Archives and Records Administration*

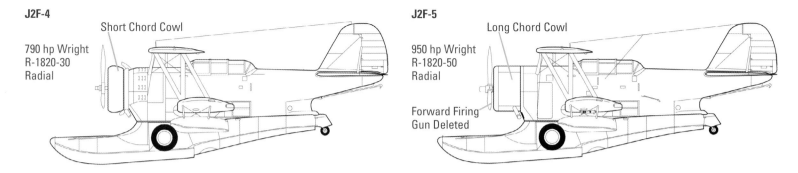

J2F-4

790 hp Wright
R-1820-30
Radial

Short Chord Cowl

J2F-5

950 hp Wright
R-1820-50
Radial

Long Chord Cowl

Forward Firing
Gun Deleted

The primary external difference between the J2F-4 and the J2F-5 is illustrated in this drawing: the short-chord cowl on the J2F-4, which tapered toward the rear, and the long-chord cowl of the J2F-5, which maintained a constant height from front to rear.

The first J2F-5 at the time this photograph was taken had a single US national insignia on top of the upper port wing. This aircraft presumably was painted NS blue-gray over NS light gray, with the latter color showing under the horizontal stabilizer. *National Archives and Records Administration*

The pilot's instrument panel of the J2F-5 was similar in design to the instrument panels of preceding models of the Duck. The small, light-colored panel between the upper and lower panels of the instrument panel held a control handle for a fire extinguisher. *National Archives and Records Administration*

The Wright R-1820-50 Cyclone engine (top) and the engine-accessories compartment of a J2F-5 are observed from above. At the bottom is the oil tank. Between the oil tank and the rear of the engine is the carburetor air intake. On top of the intake is a small decal that reads "Holley Engineered Air Scoop" and "Holley Carburetor Company USA." Also visible is part of the engine-support assembly and the exhausts. *National Archives and Records Administration*

The aft cockpit is viewed facing forward, with the rear cockpit hood slid forward, toward the top. At the bottom is the observer's seat and safety belt. Below the rear cockpit hood are the observer's flight instruments. Under the flight instruments is the radio transmitter, below which are the rudder pedals and the socket for the control stick. To the front of the right console is the radio transmitter key, for sending Morse-code messages. *National Archives and Records Administration*

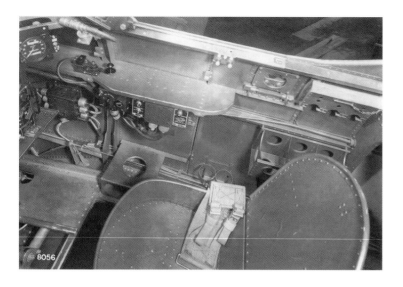

The radio transmitter on the observer's right console at the upper left is viewed from another angle. Next to the seat is a rack for storing .30-caliber ammunition boxes. Above the rack is a small door with a coil spring at the bottom for mounting the drift sight. *National Archives and Records Administration*

Mounted under the lower port wing of a J2F-5 is a Mk.41 bomb rack. A US Navy Bureau of Ordnance data plate is near the front of the rack. Two sway braces are on the bottom of the rack, one toward the front of the rack and the other toward the rear. *National Archives and Records Administration*

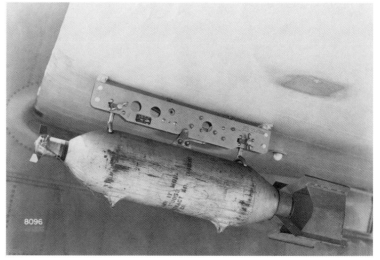

On the left side of the observer's cockpit are a rack for .30-caliber ammunition boxes and a small door for the drift sight, similar in location to the same features on the right side of the cockpit. At the center above the seat is the mount for the trailing antenna reel. *National Archives and Records Administration*

A bomb fitted with a fuse is shackled to the bomb rack. A single lug on the bomb was secured to the bomb-release mechanism on the bottom of the bomb rack. The sway braces were snugged-down to the bomb to keep it from shifting around in the rack. *National Archives and Records Administration*

A J2F-5 in early war markings flies a mission carrying aerial depth charges, or depth bombs, on the underwing racks. Grumman Ducks proved adept at antisubmarine patrolling, and a well-placed depth charge could destroy an enemy submarine. *National Museum of Naval Aviation*

A J2F-5 has an impeller for a target-towing apparatus and is armed with aerial depth charges in late April 1942. The paint scheme was NS blue-gray over NS light gray, with red and white stripes on the rudder. A small 30 is aft of the US insignia. *National Museum of Naval Aviation*

The same J2F-5 shown in the preceding photo is observed from the port side. The color of the cowl is of a slightly different tone than the fuselage. The preceding photo was credited to Utility Squadron 2, so this J2F-5 probably was assigned to that squadron. *National Museum of Naval Aviation*

On an early-production J2F-5 assigned to VJ-4 photographed around 1941, the round opening for the oil-cooler air intake is prominent between the engine exhausts below the cowling. The front tip of the center float is of a different shade than the rest of the float. *National Museum of Naval Aviation*

In the late spring of 1942, a J2F-5 of Marine Utility Squadron 153 (VMF-153) proceeds along on a dusty taxiway at Camp Kearny near San Diego. The large national insignia on the fuselage was often seen on Navy and Marine aircraft early in World War II. *National Museum of Naval Aviation*

A small number 8 is on the cowl of this J2F-5, which seems to have been assigned to duty at a US Navy photographic training base, because written on the side of the fuselage of the SNJ in the left background is "PHOTOGRAPHIC SCHOOL." *National Museum of Naval Aviation*

Cmdr. W.R. Johnson was the pilot of this J2F-5 approaching for a landing on USS *Charger* (CVE-30) on September 24, 1944. The landing signal officer (LSO) on the carrier flight deck had just waved-off Johnson, who was approaching the flight deck too high. This aircraft appears to be wearing the ASW Scheme II camouflage, with Dark Gull Gray upper surfaces and insignia white sides and gloss white undersides. *National Museum of Naval Aviation*

A J2F-5 makes an arrested landing on the escort carrier USS *Charger* (CVE-30) on August 2, 1942. The plane's arrestor hook is lowered but has not yet caught an arrestor wire. Another Grumman Duck circles in for a landing in the distance to the far right. *National Museum of Naval Aviation*

Attached to Marine Scout-Bombing Squadron 235 (VMSB-235) on Bougainville in April 1944, was this J2F-5 nicknamed *Dumbo*, with three-color camouflage of sea blue on the upper surfaces, intermediate blue on the sides, and insignia white on the lower surfaces. *National Museum of Naval Aviation*

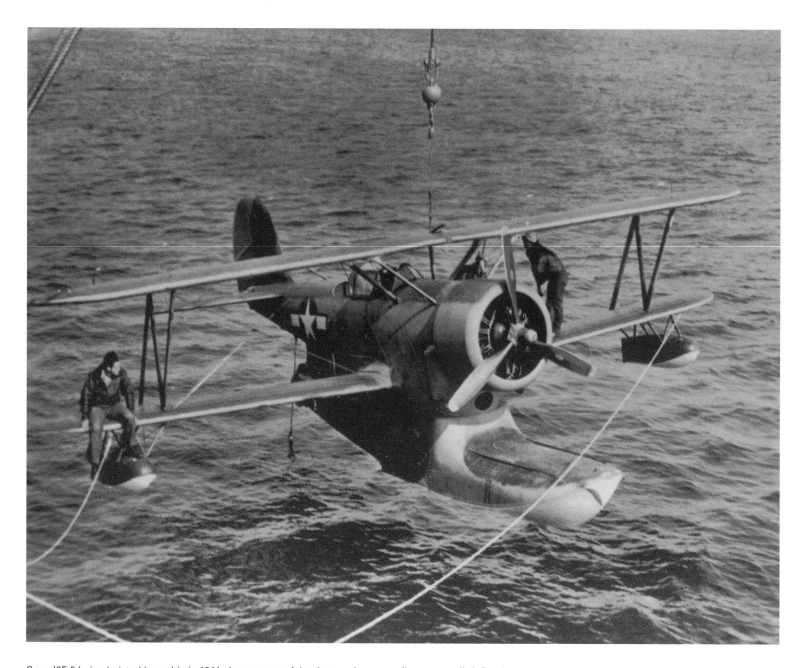

On a J2F-5 being hoisted by a ship in 1944, the patterns of the three-color camouflage are well-defined, such as the patch of sea blue on top of the forward end of the center float, and the straight line between the sea blue and intermediate blue on the fuselage. *National Museum of Naval Aviation*

CHAPTER 11
J2F-6

The last model of the Grumman Duck produced was the J2F-6. Grumman built the prototype, a modified J2F-5. To allow Grumman to concentrate on producing combat aircraft, Columbia Aircraft Co. of Valley Stream, New York, manufactured the 330 production J2F-6s. These were assigned Bureau Numbers 32637–32786, 33535–33614, and 36935–37034. The J2F-6 was very similar to the J2F-5 but was equipped with the 1,050-horsepower Wright R-1820-54 radial engine. Here, Aviation Painter 1st Class John R. Bielicki applies a coat of orange-yellow to a J2F-6 equipped for target-towing and assigned to the Atlantic Fleet Air Squadron around 1945. That color was specified as the overall color for target-towing aircraft as well as primary trainers in USN Specification SR-2e of June 1944. *Naval History and Heritage Command*

Using the Navy's standard aircraft classification code, one would expect that the J2F-6, with 330 constructed, far and away the most-produced version of the Duck to be built by Grumman, as were its predecessors. However, in fact Grumman built only one of the type—the first one. The remainder of the J2F-6 Ducks were built by Columbia Aircraft in Valley Stream, Long Island, New York. The Columbia Aircraft Ducks, built under license from Grumman, should have been designated JL-1 in keeping with standard Navy practice, but instead retained their Grumman-like designation J2F-6.

While the J2F-6 externally appears nearly identical to the J2F-5, inside the cowl of the later model is a Wright R-1820-54 Cyclone, developing 1,050 horsepower, a fifty-percent increase over the rating of the engine installed in the XJF-1.

Grumman's production lines were desperately needed for production of torpedo bombers and, more importantly fighters, leading to the J2F-6 production being shifted to Columbia Aircraft. Columbia began delivering the amphibians, which wore Bureau Numbers 32637 through 32786, 33535 through 33614, and 36935 through 37034, in early 1942. J2F-6 production was discontinued in August 1945.

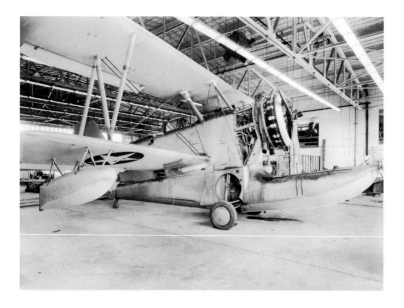

Grumman J2F-5 BuNo 00669, the prototype of the J2F-6, was equipped with a Hamilton Standard constant-speed propeller. On the J2F-6s, the Hamilton Standard Hydromatic propeller with a dome-shaped pitch-changer housing on the hub would be substituted. *Grumman Memorial Park*

Stenciled on the rudder of the prototype of the J2F-6 was "J2F-5," and on the vertical fin, "NAVY/00669" was stenciled. The clear panels and horizontal frame members in the passengers' windows have been removed. The tail wheel and caster are turned to the side. *Grumman Memorial Park*

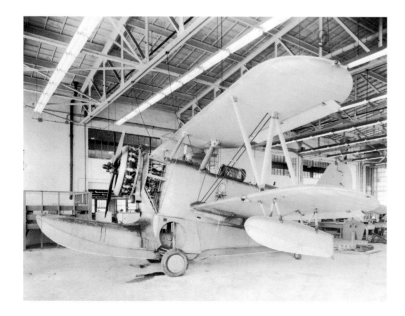

Installed on J2F-6 BuNo 00669 while it was being modified to the J2F-6 prototype was a target-towing impeller. Other details that are visible include the navigation light on the tip of the upper wing and the landing light on the leading edge of the lower wing. *Grumman Memorial Park*

From this angle, the target-towing impeller is clearly discernible alongside the pilot's cockpit. The arrestor hook had been removed from this aircraft, but the trailing-antenna fairlead is present above the upper rear corner of the passenger's window. *Grumman Memorial Park*

Photographed in December 1943, Columbia J2F-6 BuNo 36935 was the first plane in the third and final block of J2F-6 Bureau Numbers, which included 36935 to 37034. The Hamilton Standard Hydromatic propeller has the characteristic dome on the hub. *Naval History and Heritage Command*

On December 18, 1943, J2F-6 Bureau Number 36935 was photographed at NAS Patuxent River, Maryland. The Hamilton Standard Hydromatic propellers sometimes also were seen on late J2F-5s. The blades were finished in black with yellow tips. *Naval History and Heritage Command*

A J2F-6 in flight exhibits a three-color camouflage scheme. The sea blue on top of the wings continued under the leading edges of the wings, overlapping the insignia white on the undersides of the wings. Insignia white was also present on the bottoms of the floats. *National Museum of Naval Aviation*

A Columbia J2F-6 is viewed from aft at NAS Patuxent River, Maryland, on December 18, 1943. The hinged fairings on each side of the tail landing gear are visible; there was a gap between the rears of the fairings. The low profile of the canopy is visible from this angle. *Naval History and Heritage Command*

As the engine warms up, the pilot of Bureau Number 32640, an aluminum-finished J2F-6 with markings on its fuselage for its home base, NAS Atlantic City, New Jersey, checks the movement of the elevators. An antiglare panel is painted forward of the windscreen. *National Museum of Naval Aviation*

This is very likely the same J2F-6 shown in the preceding photograph, viewed from the port side. A small whip antenna is on the turtle deck between the canopy and the vertical fin. The Bureau Number is in very small figures on the vertical fin, too small to read. *National Museum of the United States Air Force*

A J2F-6 with an aluminum paint job rests on a tarmac at a desert airfield. A band is painted along the center float at the waterline, and the landing light has been moved from its original position on the leading edge of the lower port wing to underneath that wing. *National Museum of the United States Air Force*

J2F-6 BuNo 36967 flies over Southern California in 1945. It featured an aluminum finish, with wing tops painted, according to several sources, a shade of blue. A small letter Z is on the vertical fin, while the number 131 is applied roughly to the cowl. *Tailhook Association*

In a photo dated July 17, 1945, a J2F-6 flies over the Pacific in the vicinity of Hawaii Territory. This Duck is thought to have been assigned to Utility Squadron 1. In the rear cockpit, the observer, who also served as photographer and radioman, holds a camera. *National Museum of Naval Aviation*

Photographed at the Naval Air Test Center (NATC) at Patuxent River, Maryland, in late March 1949, was J2F-6 BuNo 32741. The aircraft was painted sea blue overall, and the national insignia is the type with the red stripes on the white bars adopted in 1947. *National Museum of Naval Aviation*

Another of the very few J2Fs that remain in flyable condition is *Candy Clipper*, a restored Columbia Aircraft J2F-6 Duck, USN Bureau Number 33549, manufactured in 1945, and at the time of writing owned by Kermit Weeks. It has been restored and painted to represent an earlier model of Grumman Duck named *Candy Clipper,* which operated in the Philippines in the early days of World War II. *Bill Scheuerman*

The National Museum of Naval Aviation, Pensacola, Florida, preserves Columbia J2F-6 BuNo 33581 as a static display aircraft. It is painted overall in a glossy aluminum finish, with the number 149 applied to the cowl and to the fuselage to the rear of the aft cockpit. *David Doyle*

There is a noticeable bulge in the rear edge of the lower engine-accessory-compartment access panel, to the front of the lower wing and above the main landing gear wheel, which provided an air outlet. This feature apparently was introduced with the J2F-6. *David Doyle*

With the starboard landing gear retracted, the fairing attached to the lower drag link of the landing gear fills the gap in the center float at the bottom of the wheel well. A black line on the float marks the waterline, and a vertical red stripe warns of the propeller. *David Doyle*

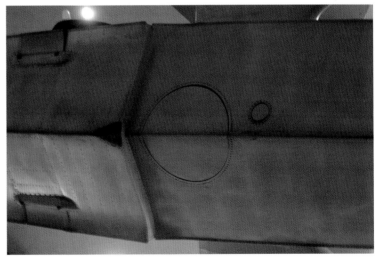

The large circle on the bottom of the center float, aft of the step of the float, was a hatch for aiming an aerial camera out of. This hatch also could be used when the plane was configured for towing a target sleeve, for feeding the sleeve and the cable out of. *David Doyle*

The empennage of the J2F-6 at the National Museum of Naval Aviation is observed from the starboard side, showing the arrestor hook and the strut between the vertical fin and the horizontal stabilizer. "DO NOT PUSH HERE" is stenciled on the fuselage tail cone. *David Doyle*

The empennage of the National Museum of Naval Aviation's Columbia J2F-6 is observed from below, showing the horizontal stabilizers, the elevators, and the elevator trim tabs. At the top center is the tail landing gear at the rear of the center float. *David Doyle*

On the arrestor hook of the J2F-6, the pivot-mount is to the right and the hook at the end of the shaft is to the left. As utility aircraft, Grumman Ducks sometimes landed on aircraft carriers, and the arrestor hook was necessary to stop the plane on the flight deck. *David Doyle*

A view of the J2F-6 from the aft port quarter gives a good idea of how the two diagonal struts on the empennage provided added rigidity for the vertical and horizontal tails. Stenciled on the elevator trim tabs is the warning, "DO NOT PUSH HERE." *David Doyle*

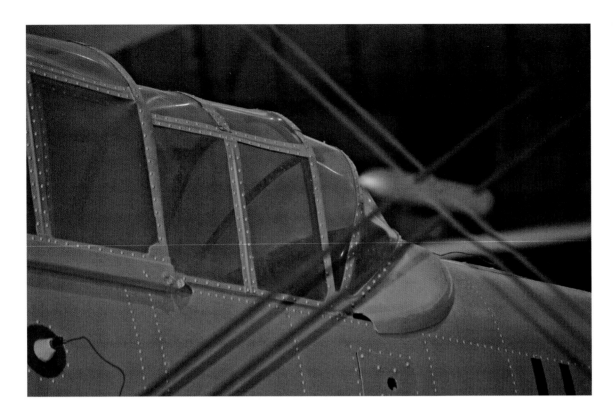

The center-to-aft portion of the canopy is observed from the port side, with the pilot's sliding section of the canopy to the left. To the center are the sliding section of the canopy over the aft cockpit and, aft of it, the rear section of the canopy, called the hood. *David Doyle*

The forward edge of the sliding section of canopy over the pilot's cockpit had a faceted, rather than rounded, shape, to match the shape of the rear edge of the windscreen when the canopy was closed. The pilot's headrest is visible within the sliding canopy. *David Doyle*

Features visible in this view of the port side of the rear of the J2F-6 include the tail wheel at the rear of the center float and the hinged tail-wheel fairing, the outline of the ribs on the rudder, and the angle of the depressed elevator at the rear of the horizontal fin. *David Doyle*

The center and forward parts of the port side of the fuselage of the J2F-6 are observed, along with details of the port wing float and wing tip. The pilot's sliding canopy is in the open position, and below the passenger's window is a step built onto the top of the float. *David Doyle*

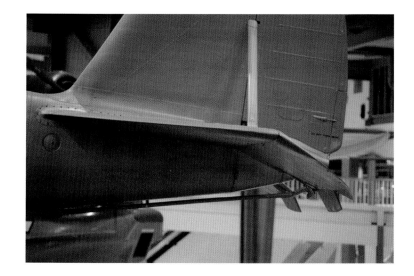

The rudder trim tab is at the bottom of the trailing edge of the rudder. Visible in this photo is the actuating link for the trim tab, which extends from a small, streamlined fairing on the side of the vertical fin to a connection near the leading edge of the trim tab. *David Doyle*

Standing vertically between the forward and the aft angled cabane struts is the single vertical cabane strut introduced with the J2F-1. At the center of the photo is the access cover for the auxiliary fuel tank filler, which had a capacity of sixty-five gallons of 100-octane. *David Doyle*

The instrument panel dominates the pilot's cockpit in the J2F-6. Below the panel are the rudder pedals; at the center is the control column, which appears to have been secured to the instrument panel with a U-shaped bracket. The throttle quadrant is to the lower left. *National Museum of the United States Air Force*

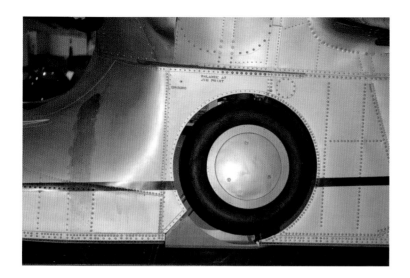

In a view of the port main landing gear in the retracted position, the fairing attached to the lower drag link is below the wheel and is a slightly different shade than the surrounding skin of the center float. The hub cap is attached with three slotted screws. *David Doyle*

Numerous features of the undersides of the lower port wing, the port wing float, and the upper wing are discernible. The landing light recessed in the lower port wing was characteristic of the J2F-6 and replaced the earlier unit in the leading edge of the wing. *David Doyle*

Two small stencils are on the float above the wheel well. The forward one reads "GROUND" and indicates a connection point for a grounding wire, essential for safety when fueling the plane. The other stencil reads "BALANCE AT JIG POINT." *David Doyle*

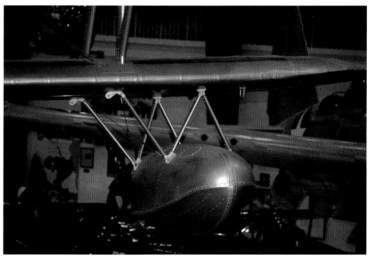

The port wing float of the J2F-6 is viewed from the front. Typically, both of the wing floats did not rest on the surface at the same time when the plane was on the water; their purpose was to help balance the plane, most of whose weight rested on the center float. *David Doyle*

The port side of the cowl and the port engine accessories compartment access panels immediately aft of the cowl are secured in place with slotted screws. The bulge formed by the lower engine accessories compartment panel was peculiar to the J2F-6. *David Doyle*

A frontal view of the J2F-6 conveys an idea of the snubbed nose of the center float and the curved shape of the exhaust tail pipes. The yellow dome on the Hamilton Standard Hydromatic propeller hub was the housing for the pitch-changing mechanism. Oval-shaped Hamilton Standard logotype decals are on the propeller blades. It can be seen how the main landing-gear wheels jutted out slightly from the sides of the center float when retracted. *David Doyle*

The J2F-6 employed the Wright R-1820-54 Cyclone radial engine with nine cylinders in a single row. Immediately aft of the propeller hub is the gear-reduction housing, encircling that housing is the ignition-harness ring, and below the housing is the oil sump. *David Doyle*

The US Army Air Forces and, later, the US Air Force, acquired a number of Grumman Ducks during and after World War II, designating them OA-12s. The first was former J2F-5 BuNo 00660, which operated mainly in the North Atlantic from 1942, until it was relegated to surplus in 1945. Five Columbia OA-12s, formerly J2F-6s, serial numbers 48-563 to 48-567, served in Alaska with the 10th Air Rescue Group. Serial number 48-563 is seen here. The plane featured red paint on the tail and wings, to make the aircraft more visible in Arctic conditions. *National Museum of the United States Air Force*

During World War II, the US Army officially operated only one Duck, the result of the Navy transferring J2F-5 00660 to the Army Air Force in 1942. The Army designated the aircraft as OA-12, and assigned it serial number 42-7771. The distinction officially is important, however, as Army fliers and ground crew of the 20th Pursuit Squadron in the Philippines salvaged a Navy J2F-4, which had been abandoned. The aircraft was used to ferry critical supplies to besieged Bataan and Corregidor. Departing during the night of April 9, badly overloaded with five passengers along with the pilot, including famed Filipino diplomat Carlos Romulo, the *Candy Clipper* would be the last plane out of Bataan before it fell.

After the war, however, several more Ducks were transferred to the Air Force from surplus Navy inventory. Five J2F-6 aircraft were overhauled at Warner-Robbins Air Base in Georgia during 1947, becoming OA-12As and receiving serial numbers 48-563 through 48-567. The aircraft were used by the 10th Rescue Squadron operating from Elmendorf and Ladd Air Force Bases.

In 1948, three more J2F-6s were overhauled, becoming OA-12Bs, wearing serial numbers 48-1373 through 48-1375. These aircraft, however, were not operated by the US Air Force, but were instead transferred to Columbia under the Pan-American Treaty of Reciprocal Assistance.

J2F Duck Bureau Numbers

0162-0190	J2F-1
0780-0794	J2F-2
1195-1209	J2F-2*
1568-1587	J2F-3
1639-1670	J2F-4**
00659-00802	J2F-5***
32637-32786	J2F-6****
33535-33614	J2F-6
36935-37034	J2F-6

* 1198-1206 converted to J2F-2A
** 1640 transferred to Coast Guard, becoming V1640
*** 00660 transferred to USAAF, becoming 42-7771
**** 32769 to USAF becoming 48-653

OA-12 serial numbers

48-563 to 48-567

48-1373 to 48-1375

Columbia OA-12 serial number 48-563 pauses at an Oklahoma Air National Guard airfield *en route* to Alaska in 1948. On the turtle deck of the aircraft were a radio mast antenna and a dark-colored radio direction-finding "football" antenna. *National Museum of the United States Air Force*

Columbia OA-12 serial number 48-566 of the 10th Rescue Group is secured to a wharf at Chekatna Lake, Alaska. This OA-12 and its four sister Ducks in the 48-563 to 48-567 serial number range served at Elmendorf and Ladd Air Force Bases in Alaska. *National Museum of the United States Air Force*

The Grumman Duck provided excellent and essential service with the US Navy, Marines, Army Air Forces, and Coast Guard as a utility aircraft, photo-reconnaissance plane, scout aircraft, air-sea rescue plane, and VIP transport before, during, and after World War II. Its ability to operate from water, land, and carrier decks gave it admirable versatility. After the war, the Duck served with several foreign armed services, and many of these amphibious planes were converted to civilian use. Although sources vary on exactly how many Ducks survive, as of this writing, ten J2Fs were registered with the Federal Aviation Administration. *Bill Scheuerman*